GUT

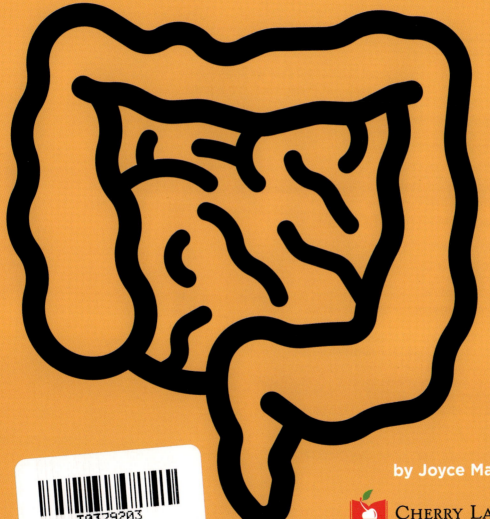

by Joyce Markovics

CHERRY LAKE PRESS
Ann Arbor, Michigan

Published in the United States of America by Cherry Lake Publishing Group
Ann Arbor, Michigan
www.cherrylakepublishing.com

Reading Adviser: Beth Walker Gambro, MS Ed., Reading Consultant, Yorkville, IL
Content Advisers: Sharon Markovics, MD, and Peter Markovics, MD
Book Designer: Ed Morgan

Photo Credits: Wikimedia Commons, 4; Wikimedia Commons, 5 top; Wikimedia Commons, 5 bottom; Wikimedia Commons, 6; © Madrock24/Shutterstock, 7; freepik.com, 8; © Olga Bolbot/Shutterstock, 9; © Liya Graphics/Shutterstock, 10; freepik.com, 11 top; freepik.com, 11 bottom; freepik.com, 12; © Aldona Grixskeviciene/Shutterstock, 13; © Ben Schonewille/Shutterstock, 14; freepik.com, 15; freepik.com, 16; Wikimedia Commons, 17; © LightField Studio/Shutterstock, 18; freepik.com, 19; © Alpha Tauri 3D Graphics/Shutterstock, 20–21.

Copyright © 2023 by Cherry Lake Publishing Group

All rights reserved. No part of this book may be reproduced or utilized in any form or by any means without written permission from the publisher.

Cherry Lake Press is an imprint of Cherry Lake Publishing Group.

Library of Congress Cataloging-in-Publication Data

Names: Markovics, Joyce L., author.
Title: Gut / by Joyce Markovics.
Description: Ann Arbor, Michigan : Cherry Lake Publishing, [2023] | Series: Hello, body! | Includes bibliographical references and index. | Audience: Grades 4-6
Identifiers: LCCN 2022003678 (print) | LCCN 2022003679 (ebook) | ISBN 9781668909591 (hardcover) | ISBN 9781668911198 (paperback) | ISBN 9781668914373 (adobe pdf) | ISBN 9781668912782 (ebook)
Subjects: LCSH: Digestive organs—Juvenile literature. | Gastrointestinal system—Juvenile literature.
Classification: LCC QP145 .M3673 2023 (print) | LCC QP145 (ebook) | DDC 612.3–dc23/eng/20220224
LC record available at https://lccn.loc.gov/2022003678
LC ebook record available at https://lccn.loc.gov/2022003679

Printed in the United States of America by
Corporate Graphics

CONTENTS

Belly Window 4
The Digestive System 8
Esophagus to Stomach 12
Interesting Intestines 16
Your Microbiome 20
   Health Tips 22
   Glossary 23
   Find Out More 24
   Index 24
   About the Author 24

BELLY WINDOW

Bang! In 1822, Alexis St. Martin felt a bullet rip through his stomach. He was working at a **trading post** in Michigan when he was accidentally shot. The gunshot tore through Alexis's muscles and ribs. No one expected him to live.

Alexis St. Martin was a healthy young man in his twenties when he was shot.

A doctor named William Beaumont treated Alexis. Remarkably, Alexis slowly recovered. However, he never fully healed. The gunshot left a hole in Alexis's side that connected to his stomach. At first, whenever Alexis swallowed food, it came spilling out of the hole!

Doctor William Beaumont

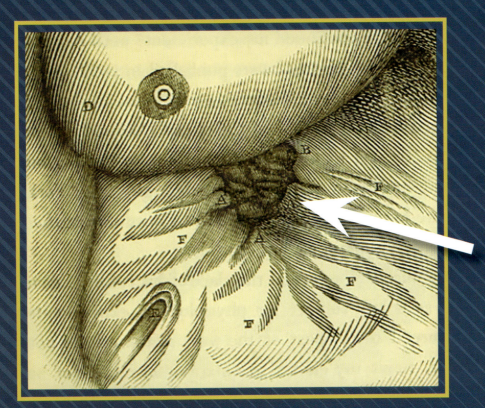

This artwork shows Alexis's stomach injury. In medical terms, it's called a fistula (FIS-chuh-luh).

After 17 days, the food stayed inside Alexis's stomach. Yet the hole remained. Dr. Beaumont saw this as a chance to learn about the human digestive system. In the early 1800s, very little was known about how the body processed food.

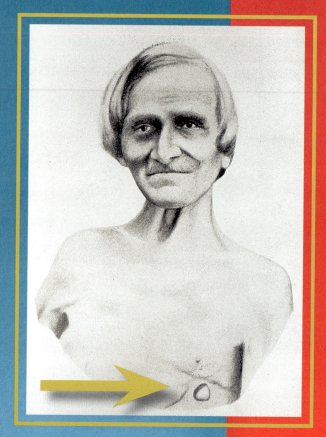

Alexis St. Martin lived to be 78.

The human digestive system is often called the gut. It includes many parts that help the body break down and absorb food.

For a decade, Dr. Beaumont closely studied Alexis. In one **experiment**, the doctor dangled food tied to a string inside the stomach hole. After a few minutes, he pulled it out to see what had been digested. Dr. Beaumont performed close to 200 experiments on Alexis. The research led to a deeper understanding of the human digestive system.

A model of a human stomach

THE DIGESTIVE SYSTEM

Think about the last time you ate something like pizza. Did your mouth start watering even before you tasted it? The digestive process begins before you ever take your first bite. And it continues after you've swallowed your last mouthful of food!

Your digestive system includes lots of body parts that work together. They turn the food and liquids that you eat and drink into the **nutrients** and energy your body needs.

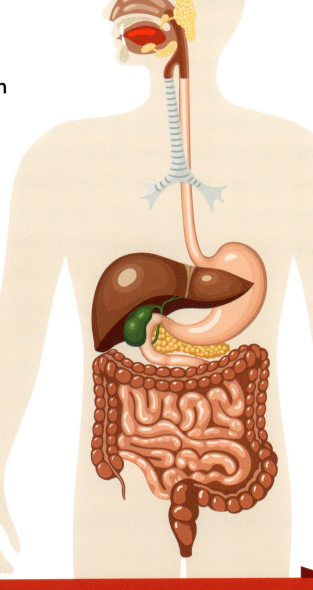

Your digestive system

People and most animals have a digestive tract, or alimentary (a-luh-MEN-tuh-ree) canal.

9

Your digestive tract is basically a long tube. It stretches from your mouth to your **anus** and is made up of different **organs**. An adult human's digestive tract is about 30 feet (9 meters) long! That's about as long as a school bus.

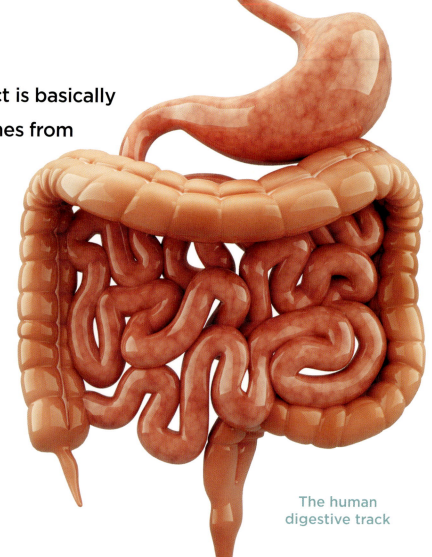

The human digestive track

Digestion starts when you see, smell, or even think about tasty food. You might produce saliva (suh-LYE-vuh). It's a watery liquid made by special **glands** in your mouth. Saliva contains **enzymes** that start breaking down food. For example, when you eat popcorn, your teeth chop it up. Then saliva breaks down and softens the popcorn, making it easy to swallow.

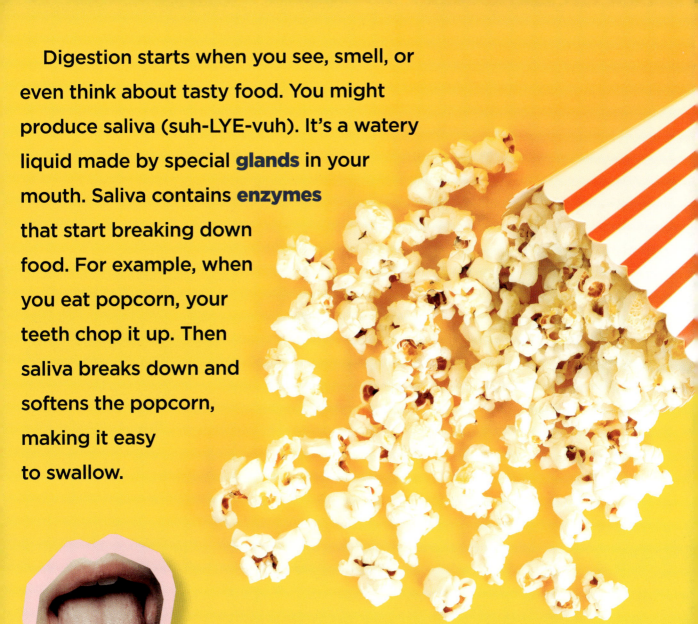

Saliva, also called spit, is 98 percent water.

ESOPHAGUS TO STOMACH

The second part of the digestive tract is the esophagus (ih-SAH-fuh-guhs). It's a stretchy 10-inch- (25-centimeter) long pipe in your throat. After you swallow, food travels from the start of the esophagus to your stomach.

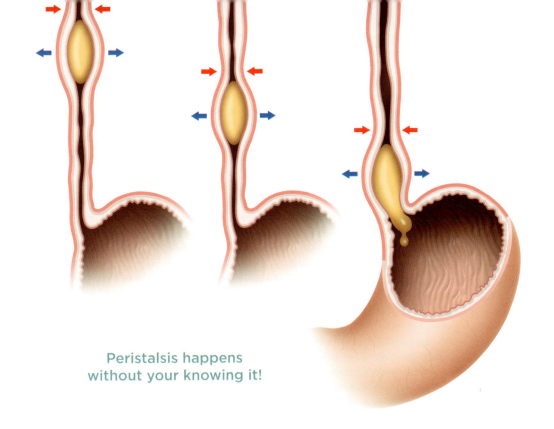

Peristalsis happens without your knowing it!

However, mushed-up food doesn't just plop into your stomach. Muscles squeeze the food in wavelike movements down your esophagus. This action is known as peristalsis (per-uh-STALL-suhs). After a few seconds, the food arrives in your stomach.

Wrong pipe! Have you ever coughed while eating or drinking too fast? Your esophagus is next to your windpipe, which is how air gets to your lungs. Sometimes, food or liquids enter your windpipe by mistake, making you cough.

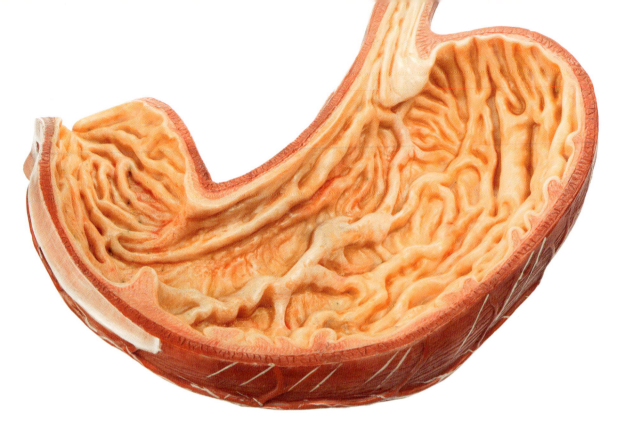

Your stomach is shaped a little like the letter *J*!

Your stomach is like a mixer inside your body. It's a stretchy, muscular sack that's filled with **gastric** juices. These so-called juices are made by the lining of the stomach. They include **acid** and other substances that help break down food.

A muscular ring separates the esophagus from the stomach. It lets food enter the stomach. But then it squeezes shut to stop your stomach contents and acid from flowing back up. When the food is ready to leave the stomach, it looks nothing like the food you swallowed! Rather, it's a thick, gooey soup called chyme (KIME).

When your stomach detects something harmful in the food you ate, you might vomit. That's one way your body protects you from illness.

Gastric juices also kill germs in your food that could make you sick.

INTERESTING INTESTINES

After leaving the stomach, chyme enters your small intestine—only it's not small. It stretches about 22 feet (6.7 m)! The small intestine has one main job. It breaks down chyme into even smaller bits. To do this, the small intestine uses tiny fingerlike parts called villi (VIH-lye).

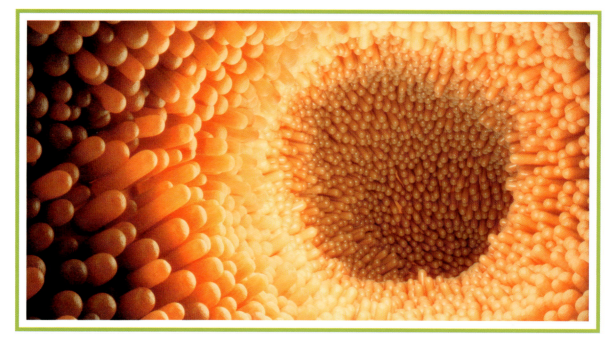

The villi of the small intestine

The walls of the small intestine are covered with millions of villi. They absorb nutrients from the chyme and pass them into your blood and to the rest of your body. Helping the small intestine are three key organs: the **pancreas**, gallbladder, and liver. They each make substances **vital** for digestion.

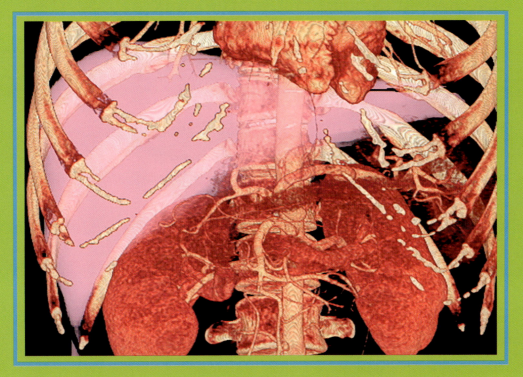

The liver is shown in pink in this image. The liver makes a greenish fluid called bile. It helps the body absorb fat. The liver also cleans the blood and stores energy.

The food you eat can spend up to 4 hours in your small intestine!

From the small intestine, what's left of the food passes to the large intestine. It's the final stop in the digestive tract. It's thicker than the small intestine but shorter—only about 5 feet (1.5 m) long. At this point, most of what remains in the large intestine is waste.

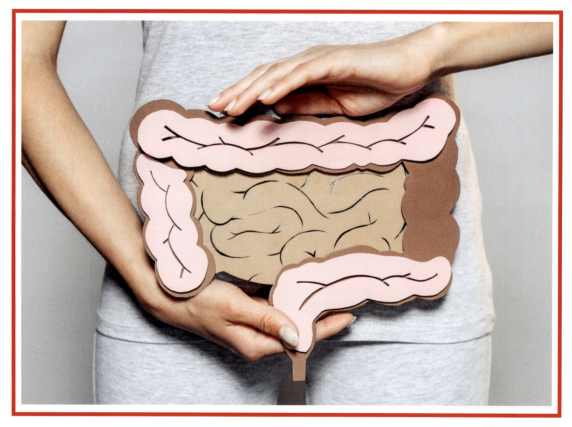

The colon absorbs salts too.

A big part of the large intestine is the colon. It absorbs water from the waste. Eventually, the waste transforms from a liquid to a brownish solid. Guess what this solid is? It's feces (FEE-seez), or poop! Feces are stored in the rectum, the final section of the large intestine. Then they get pushed out of the anus when a person goes to the bathroom. This is the last part of digestion.

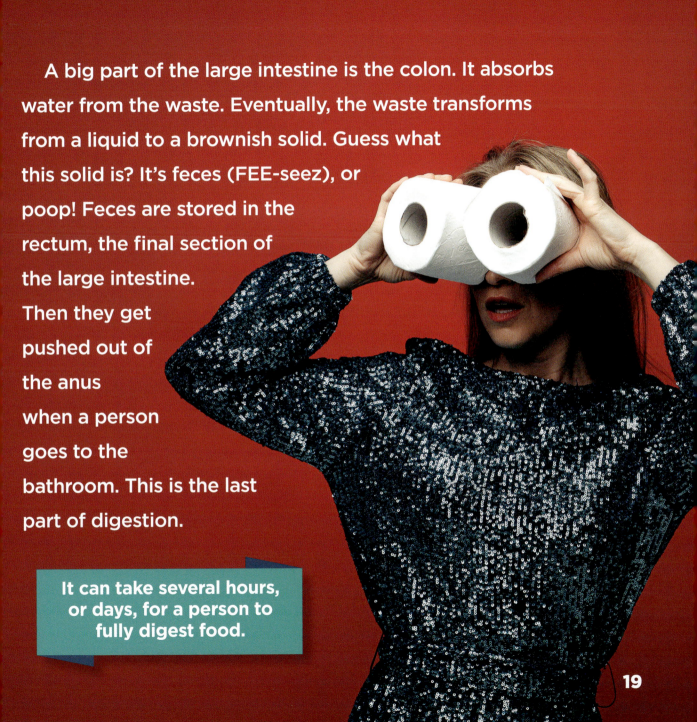

It can take several hours, or days, for a person to fully digest food.

YOUR MICROBIOME

Picture a busy city with millions of people rushing around. On a **microscopic** level, that's what the inside of your gut looks like! There are trillions of tiny living things called microbes (MYE-krohbz) living in your large and small intestines. Each person has a unique set of these tiny living things. Together, they're called your microbiome (mye-kroh-BYE-ohm).

In a healthy person, the microbes **coexist**. In fact, they can prevent and help fight illness. Sometimes, a person's microbiome can be out of balance. That person is more likely to get and stay sick. Experts are still learning about the marvelous microbiome—and how it makes you a healthier you!

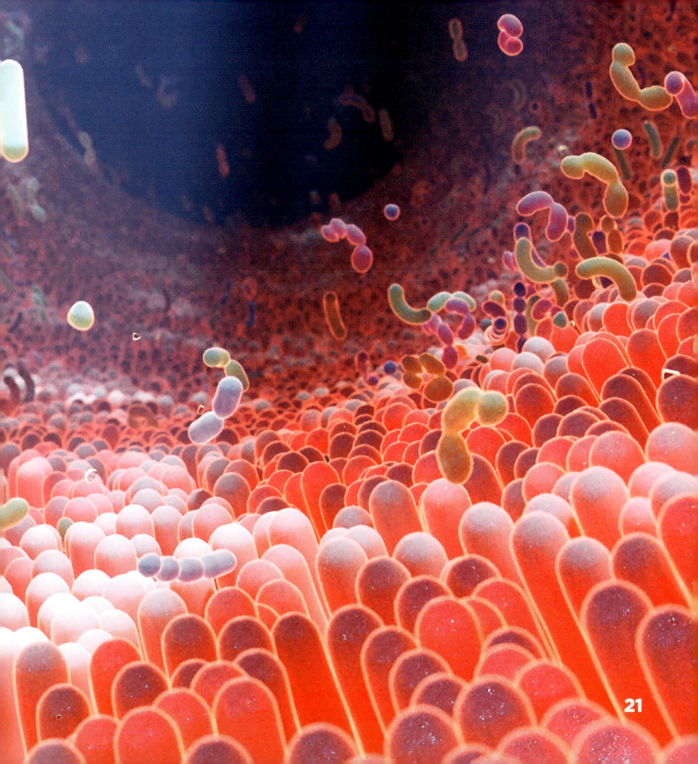

Here are some ways to keep your gut healthy:

- Drink plenty of water!

- Eat lots of fiber-rich foods, such as vegetables, fruits, and whole grains. Fiber makes it easier for feces to pass through your body.

- Be active! Exercise at least three times a week. Walk, play, bike, jump, or dance.

GLOSSARY

absorb (ab-ZORB) to soak up something

acid (AS-uhd) a chemical that can dissolve things such as metal

anus (EY-nuhs) the opening of the lower end of the digestive tract through which solid waste leaves the body

coexist (koh-ig-ZIST) to exist together peaceably

enzymes (EN-zymz) substances produced by the body that bring about changes in it

experiment (ik-SPER-uh-muhnt) a scientific test set up to find the answer to a question

gastric (GA-strik) relating to the stomach

glands (GLANDZ) body parts that produce natural chemicals

microscopic (mye-kruh-SKAH-pik) extremely tiny; able to be seen only with a microscope

nutrients (NOO-tree-uhnts) substances needed by the body to grow and stay healthy

organs (OR-guhnz) body parts that do a particular job

pancreas (PAN-kree-uhs) a large gland that produces substances needed for digestion

trading post (TRAYD-ing POHST) a store where people can trade local products for food and supplies

vital (VYE-tuhl) very important

FIND OUT MORE

BOOKS

Johnson, Rebecca L. *Your Digestive System*. Minneapolis, MN: Lerner Publications, 2013.

Simon, Seymour. *Guts: Our Digestive System*. New York, NY: HarperCollins, 2019.

Simon, Seymour. *The Human Body*. New York, NY: HarperCollins, 2008.

WEBSITES

American Museum of Natural History: The Microbiome of Your Gut
https://www.amnh.org/exhibitions/the-secret-world-inside-you/gut-microbiome

Britannica Kids: Digestive System
https://kids.britannica.com/kids/article/digestive-system/353054

National Geographic Kids: Human Digestive System
https://www.natgeokids.com/uk/discover/science/general-science/your-digestive-system/

INDEX

alimentary canal, 9
anus, 10, 19
chyme, 15–17
digestive system, 6–9
enzymes, 11
esophagus, 12–13, 15
feces, 19, 22
gastric juices, 14–15
glands, 11
large intestine, 18–19
liver, 17

microbes, 20–21
microbiome, 20–21
nutrients, 9, 17
organs, 10, 17
pancreas, 17
peristalsis, 13
saliva, 11
small intestine, 16–18, 20
St. Martin, Alexis, 4–7
stomach, 4–7, 14–17
villi, 16–17

ABOUT THE AUTHOR

Joyce Markovics has written hundreds of books for kids. She would like to thank Pete for being a wonderful gastroenterologist and expert reader. She dedicates this book to her aunt, Lee, who isn't always friends with her microbiome.